JEWISH SONGS
FOR ACCORDION

ARRANGED BY GARY MEISNER

ISBN 978-1-61780-474-8

HAL•LEONARD®
CORPORATION
7777 W. BLUEMOUND RD. P.O. BOX 13819 MILWAUKEE, WI 53213

In Australia Contact:
Hal Leonard Australia Pty. Ltd.
4 Lentara Court
Cheltenham, Victoria, 3192 Australia
Email: ausadmin@halleonard.com.au

Visit Hal Leonard Online at
www.halleonard.com

ADON OLAM
(Master of the Word)

Traditional Jewish Song

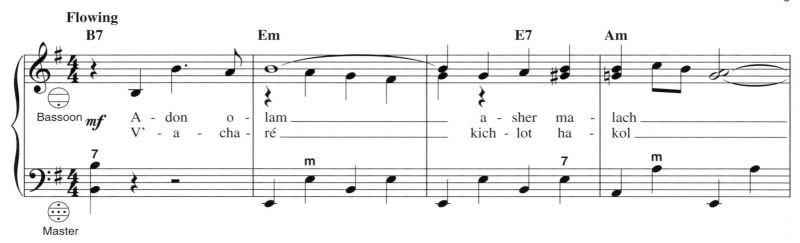

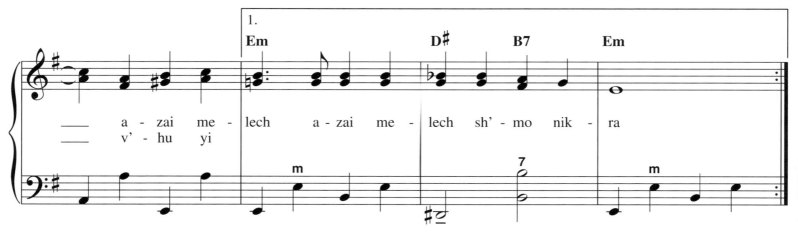

ye v'-hu yi - ye b'-tif - a - ra ___

___ a - don o - lam a - sher ma-lach b'-te - rem kol y'-tsir niv-ra l'-

ét na'a sa b'-chef-tso kol a - zai me-lech sh'-mo nik-ra v'-a-cha-ré kich-lot ha-kol ___

l'-va-do yim-loch no-ra v'-hu ha-ya v'-hu ho-ve v'-hu yi-ye b'-tuf-a-ra a-

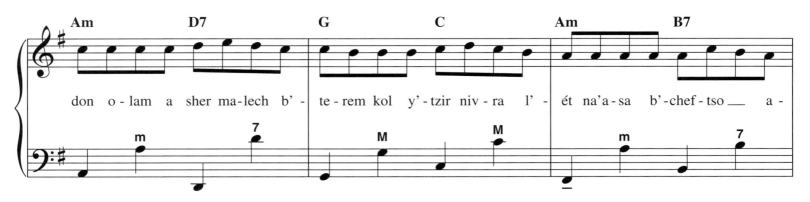

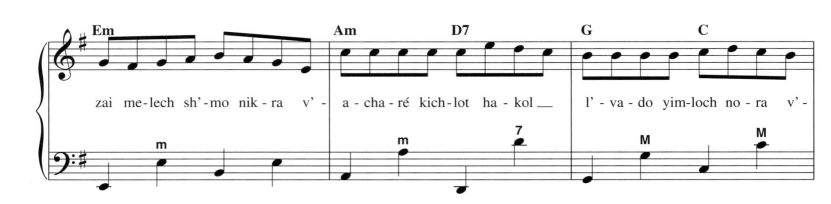

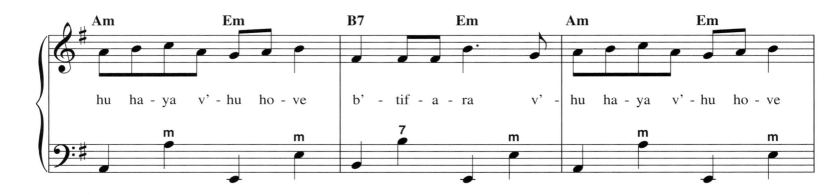

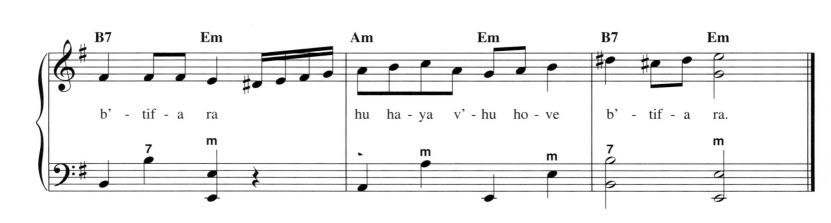

HAVA NAGILA
(Let's Be Happy)

Lyrics by MOSHE NATHANSON
Music by ABRAHAM Z. IDELSOHN

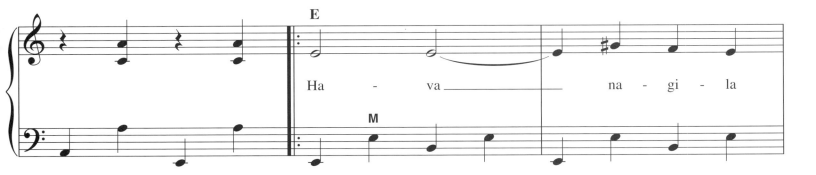

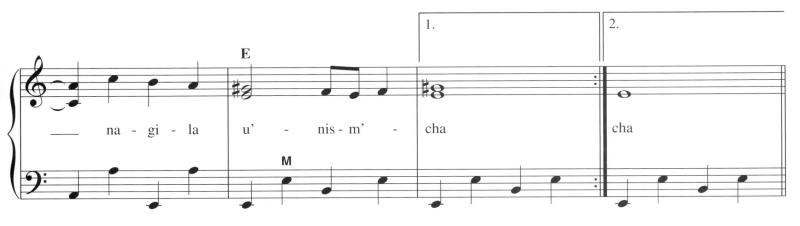

8

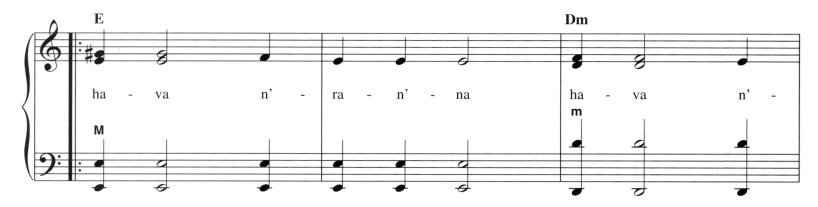

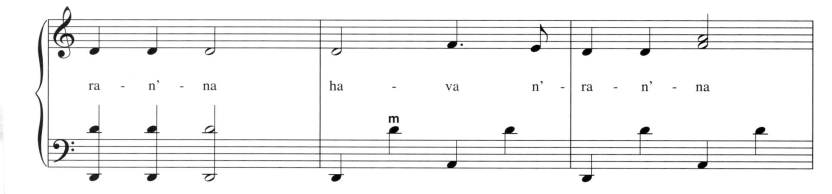

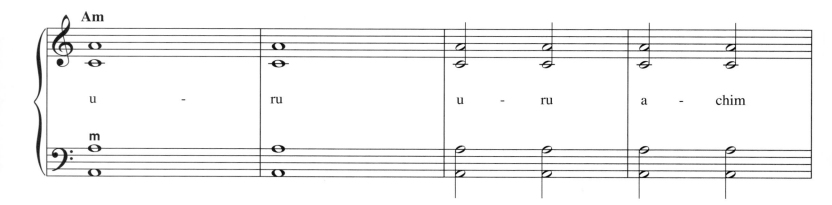

9

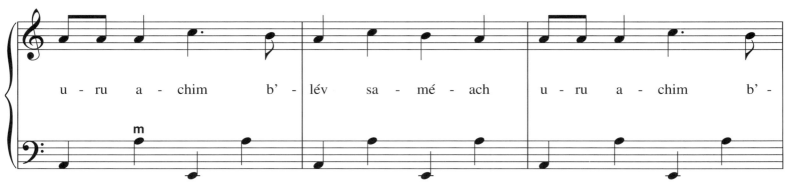

u - ru a - chim b' - lév sa - mé - ach u - ru a - chim b' -

lév sa - mé - ach u - ru a - chim b' - lév sa - mé - ach

u - ru a - chim b' - lév sa - mé - ach u - ru a - chim

u - ru a - chim b' - lév sa - mé - ach.

AMÉN SHEM NORA
(Amen, the Name of the Light)

Sephardic Folksong

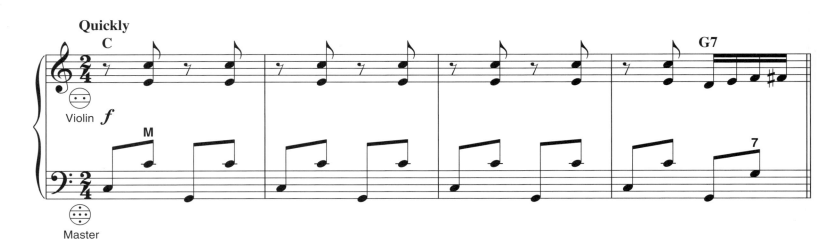

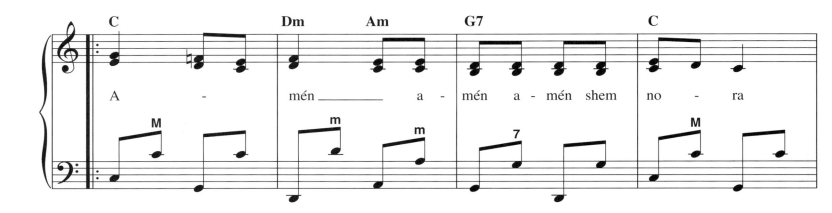

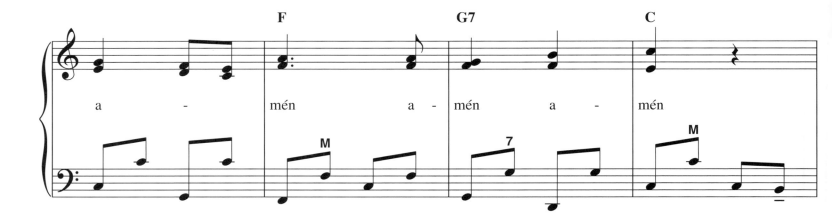

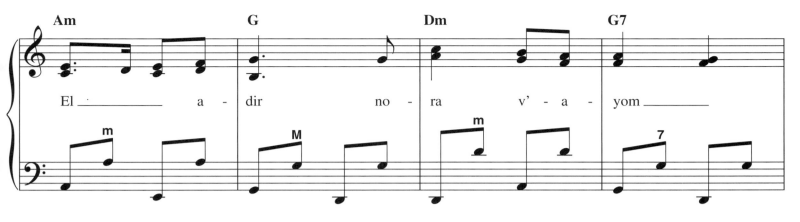

El _____ a - dir no - ra v' - a - yom _____

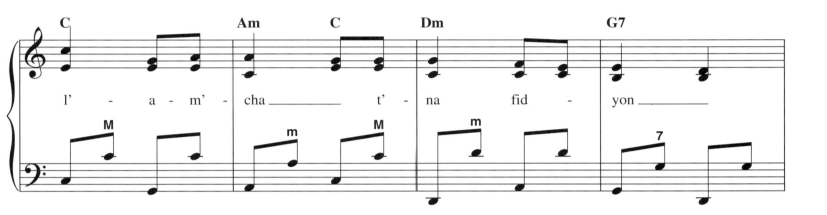

l' - a - m' - cha _____ t' - na fid - yon _____

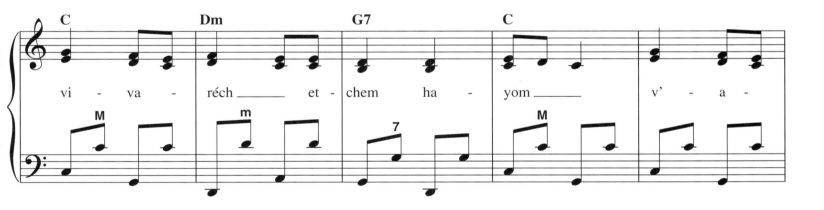

vi - va - réch _____ et - chem ha - yom _____ v' - a -

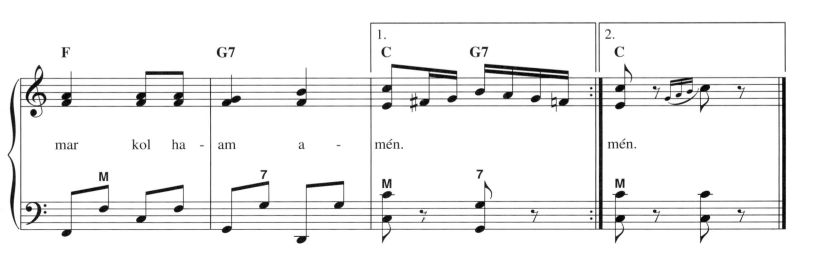

mar kol ha - am a - mén.

mén.

ARTSA ALINU

Traditional Hebrew
National Dance Of Israel

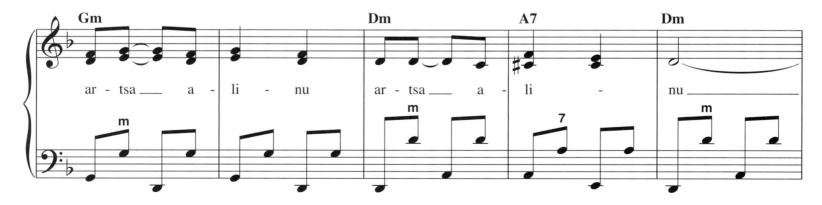

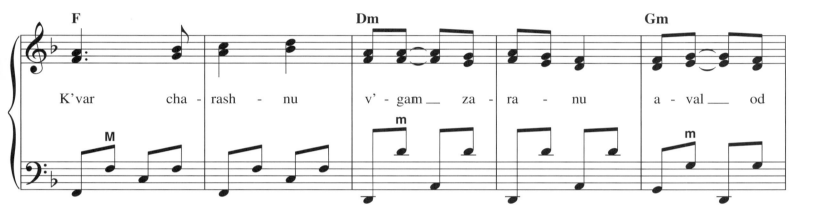

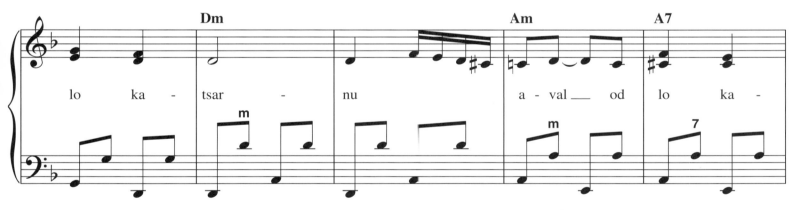

AVINU MALKÉNU
(God, Our King)

Traditional Hebrew Lyrics
Liturgical Melody

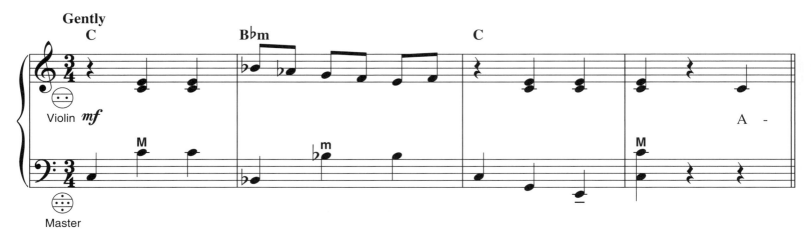

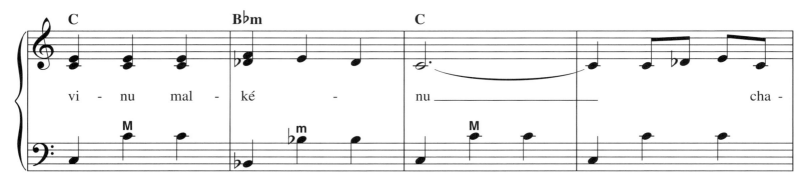

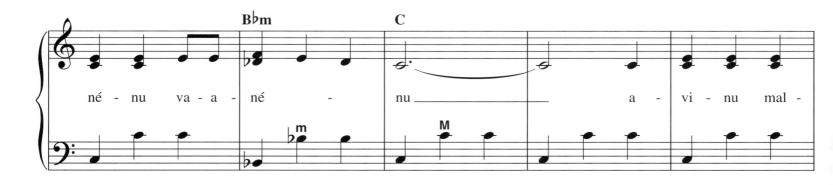

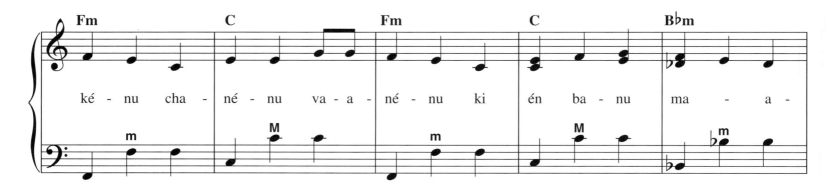

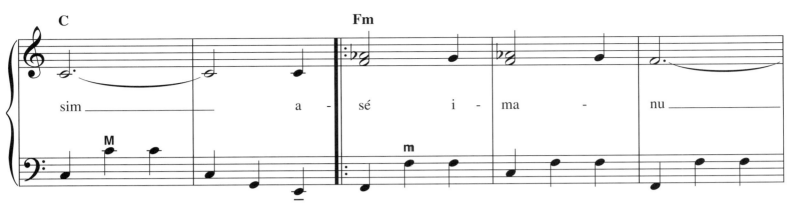

sim _____ a - sé i - ma - nu _____

_____ ts' - da - ka va - che - sed _____ a -

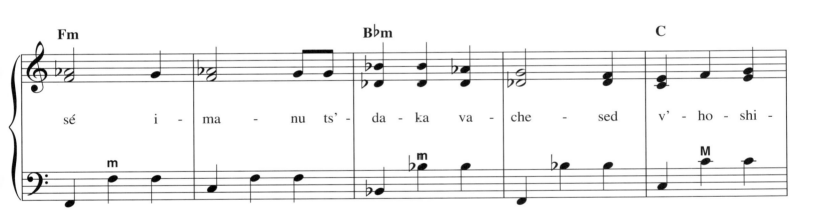

sé i - ma - nu ts' - da - ka va - che - sed v' - ho - shi -

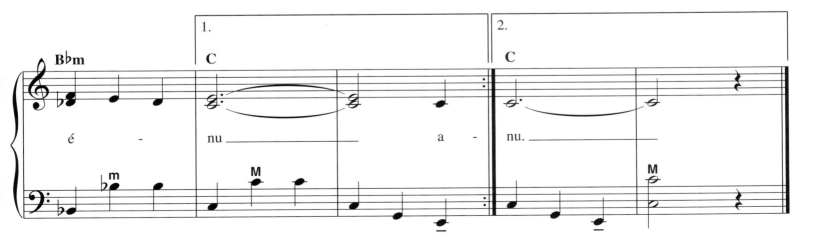

é - nu _____ a - nu.

CHOSON KALE MAZEL TOV
(Good Luck to the Bride and Groom)

Traditional Jewish Song

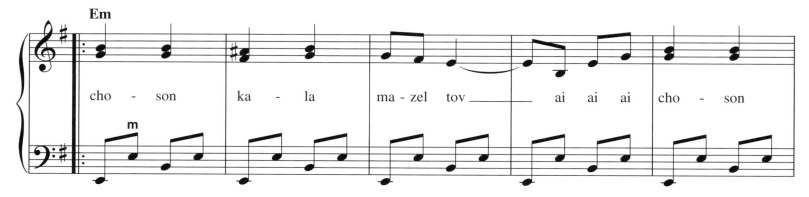

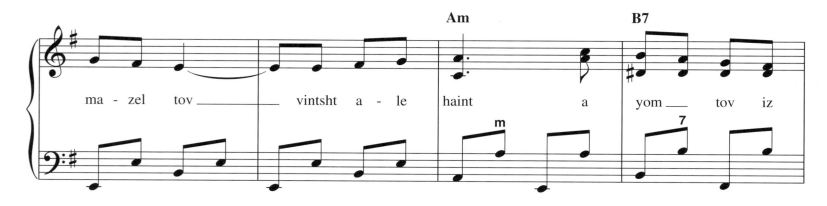

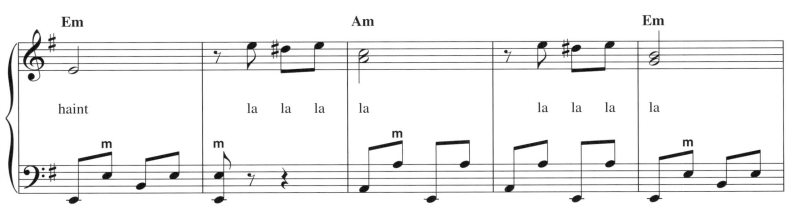

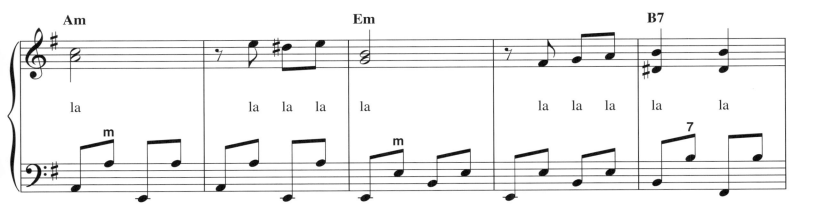

DAVID MELECH YISRAÉL

Traditional Hebrew

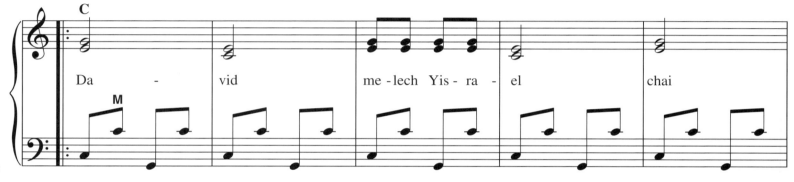

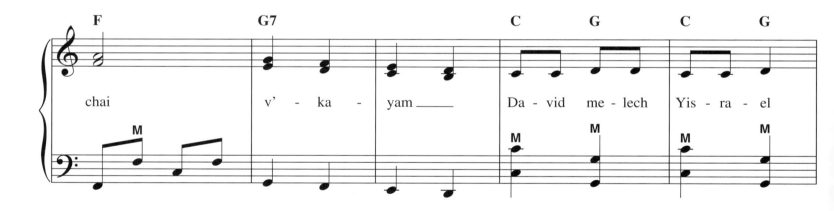

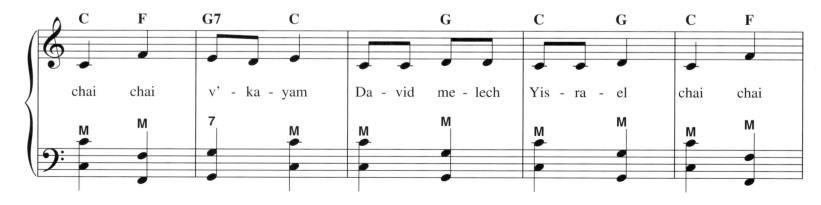

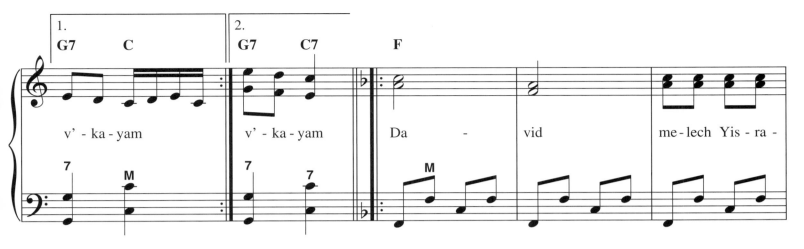

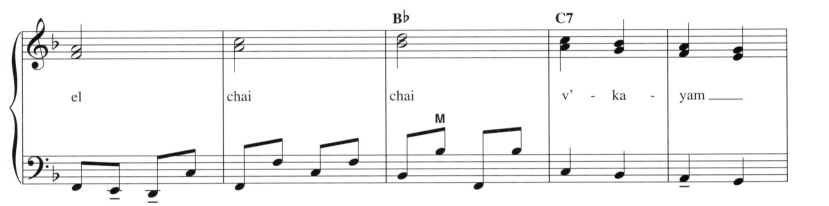

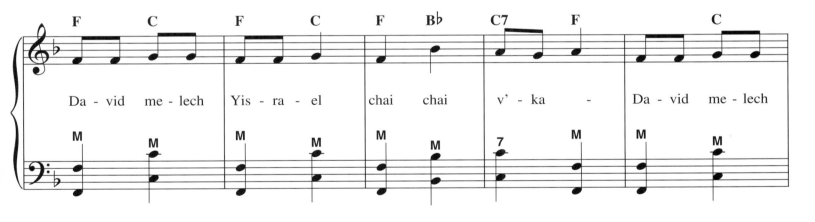

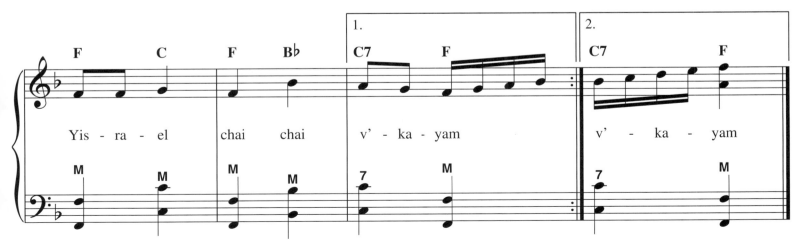

DER REBBE ÉLIMÉLECH

(The Rabbi Élimélech)

Yiddish Folksong

Az der Reb - be É - li -

mé - lech iz ge - vo - ren zé - er fré - lach iz ge - vo - ren zé - er fré - lach É - li -

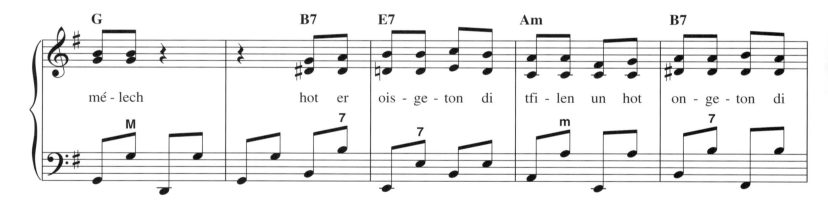

mé - lech hot er ois - ge - ton di tfi - len un hot on - ge - ton di

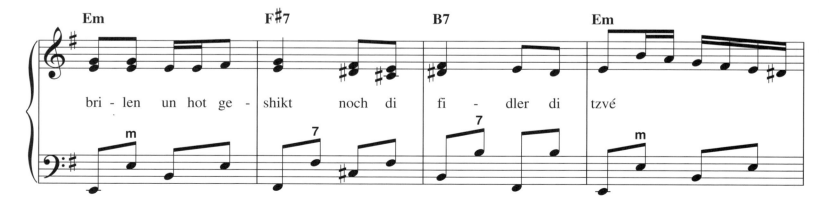

bri - len un hot ge - shikt noch di fi - dler di tzvé

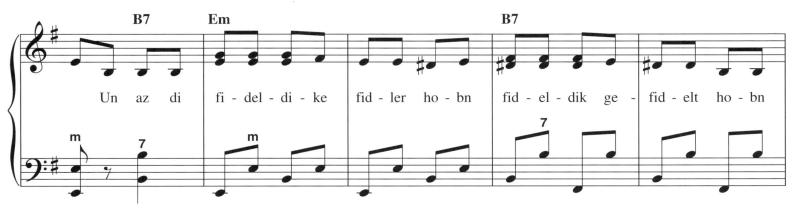

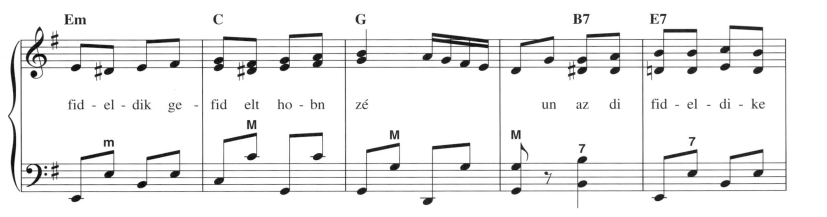

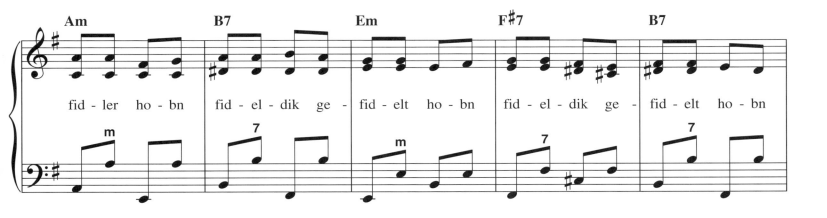

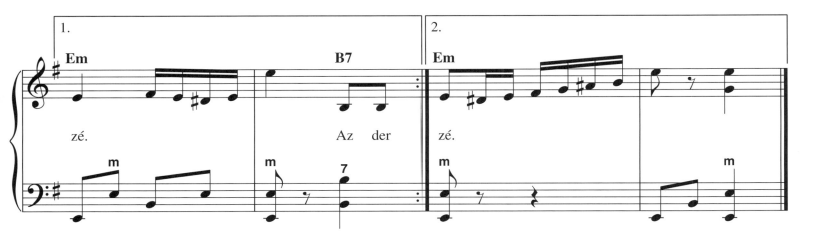

FRAILACH
(Happy)

Traditional Jewish Dance

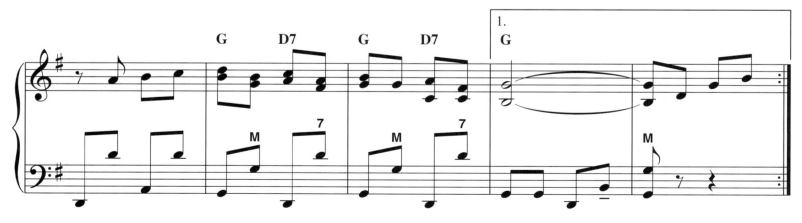

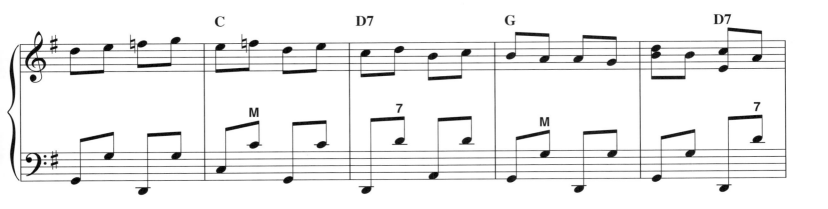

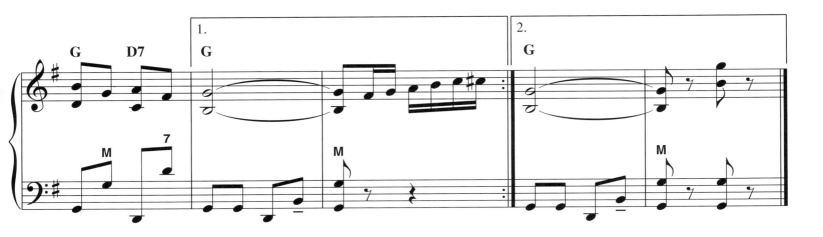

HATIKVAH
(With Hope)

Traditional Hebrew Melody
Lyrics by N.H. IMBER

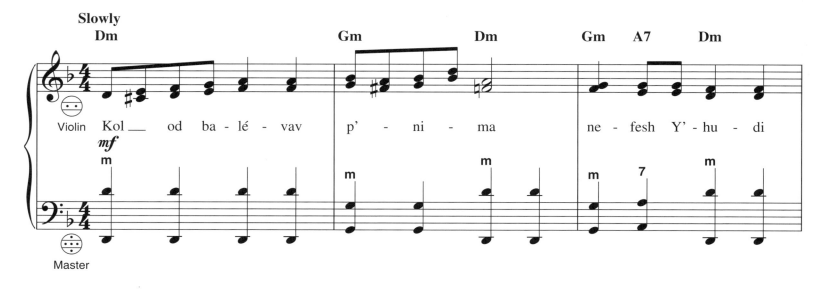

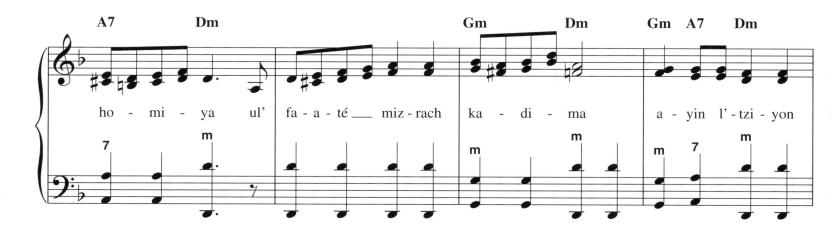

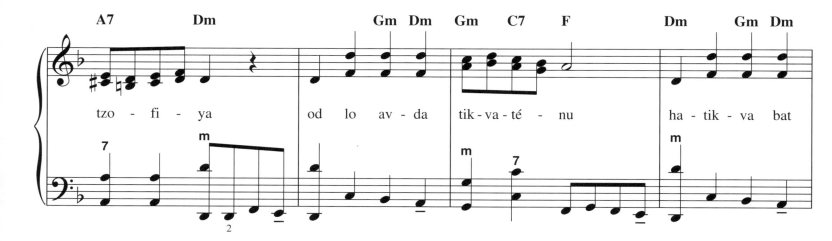

25

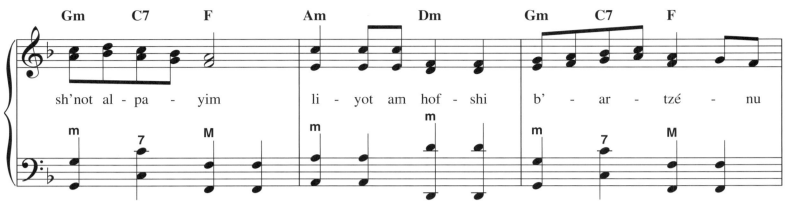

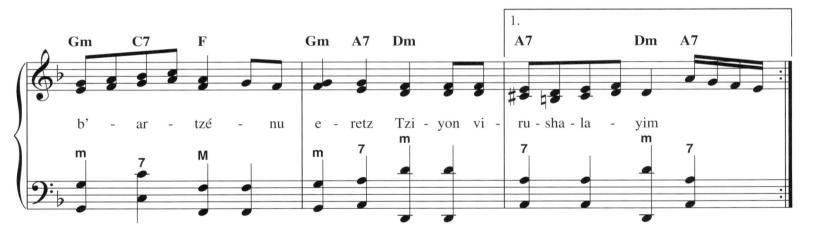

I HAVE A LITTLE DREYDL

Traditional Hebrew Folk Song

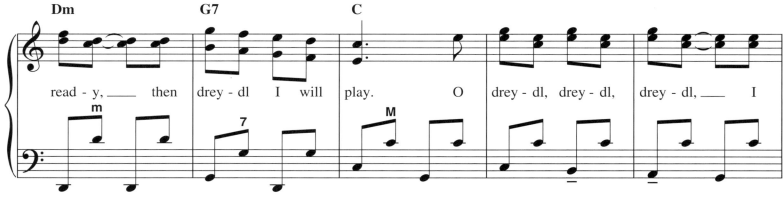

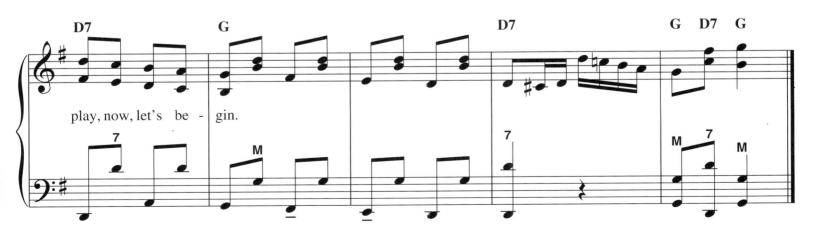

IM ESHKACHÉCH
(If I Will Ever Forget You Jerusalem)

Traditional Klezmer Song

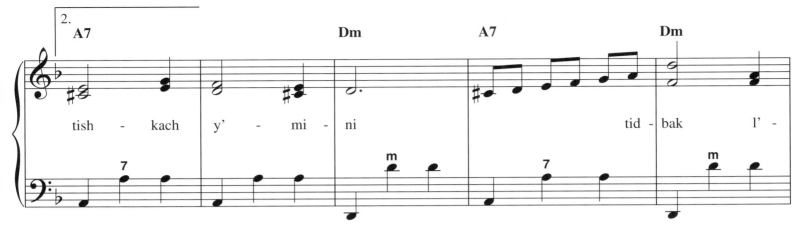

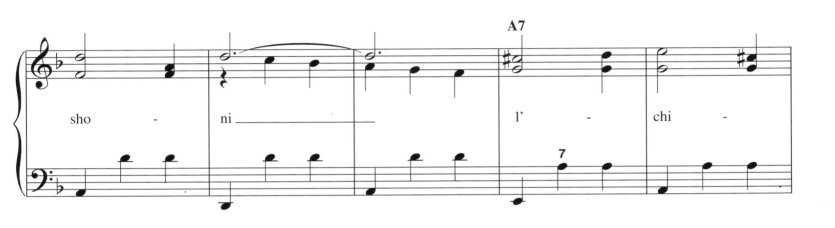

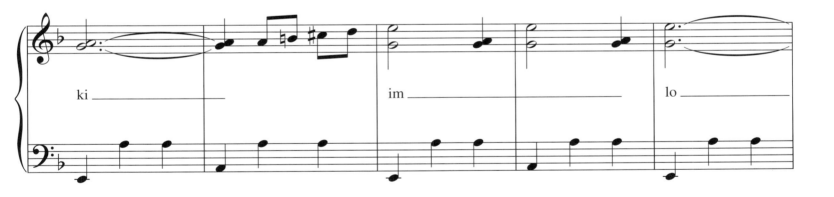

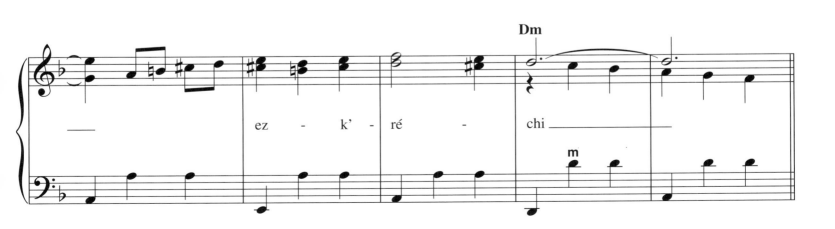

30

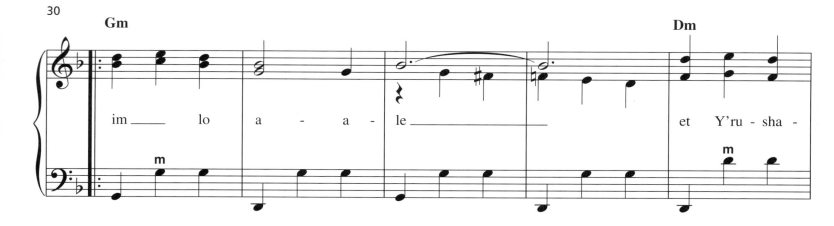

im _____ lo   a - a - le _____   et   Y'ru - sha -

la - yim _____   al _____

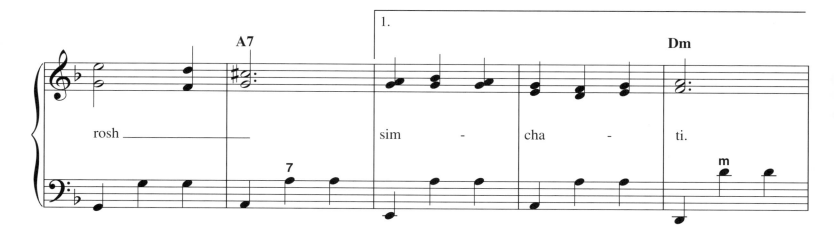

1.

rosh _____   sim - cha - ti.

2.

sim - cha - ti.

MA NISHTANA
(What Is the Difference?)

Jewish Folksong

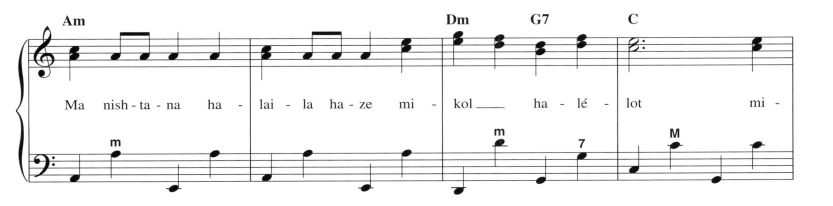

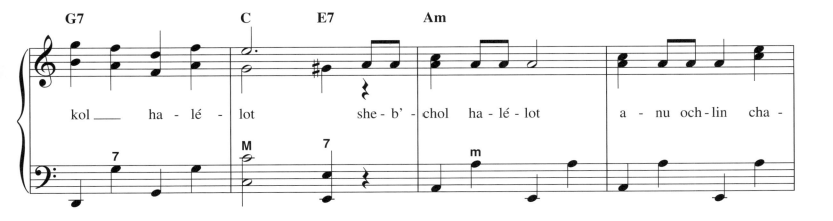

32

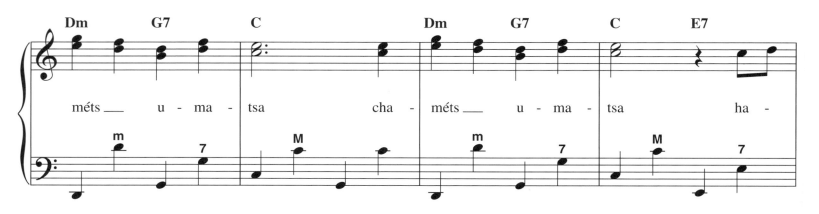

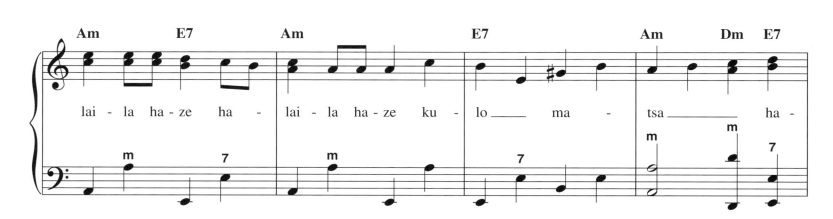

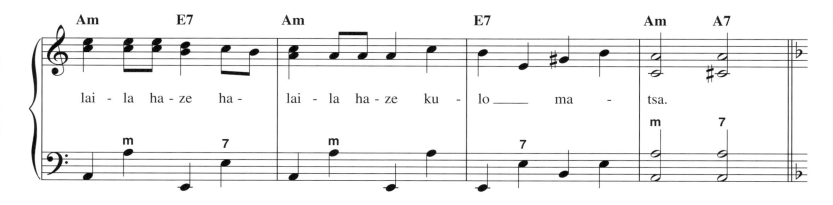

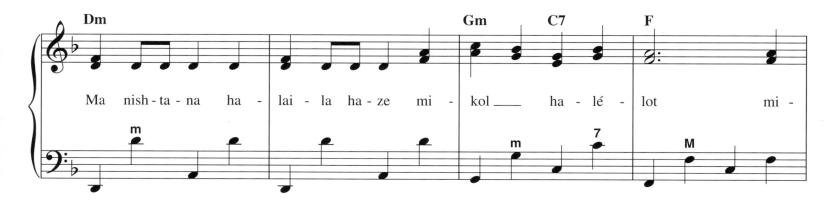

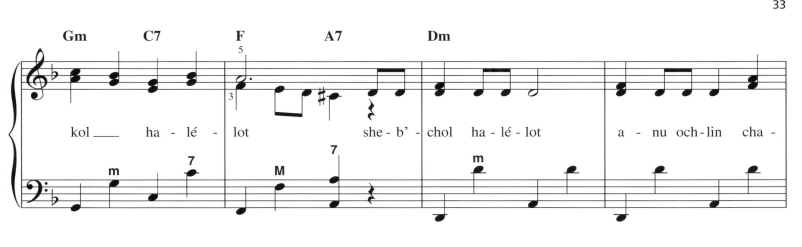

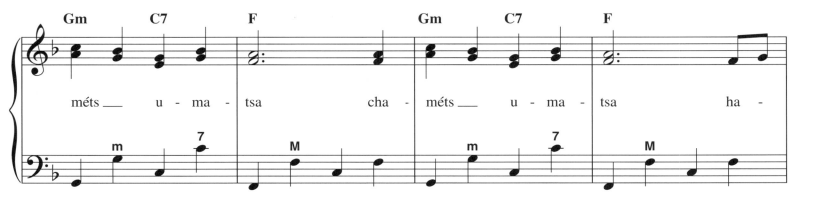

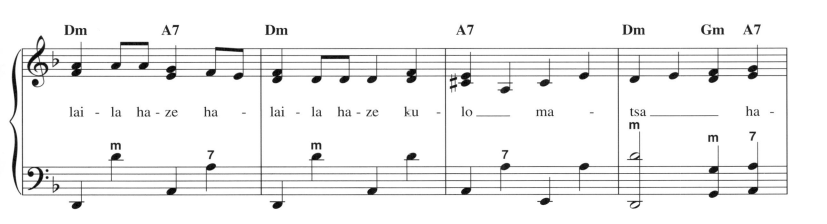

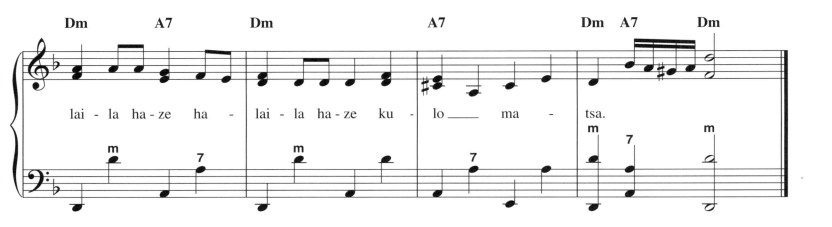

MA NAVU
(How Welcome on the Mountains)

Jewish Folksong

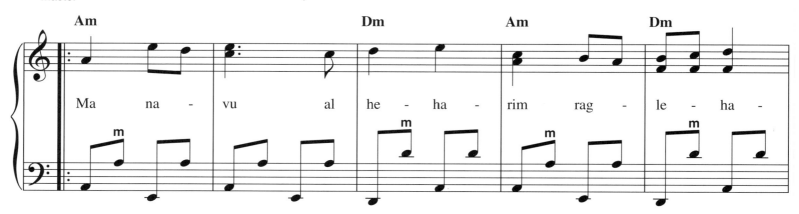

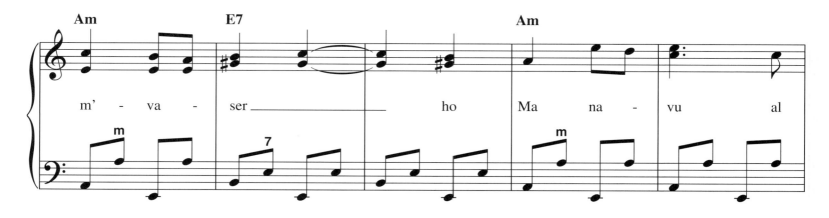

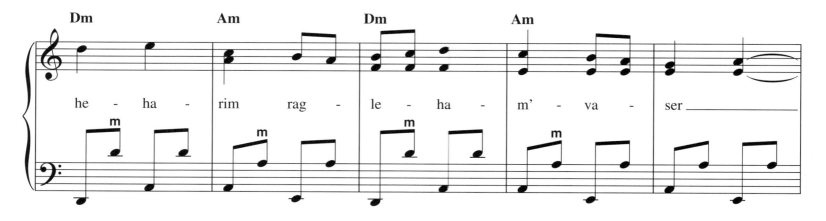

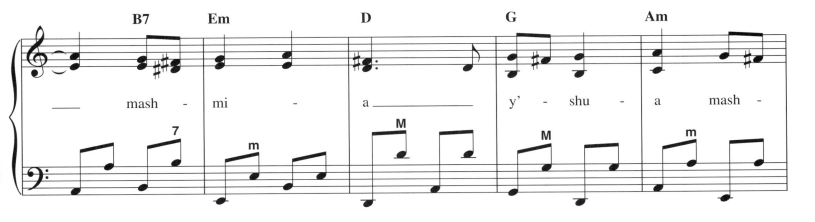

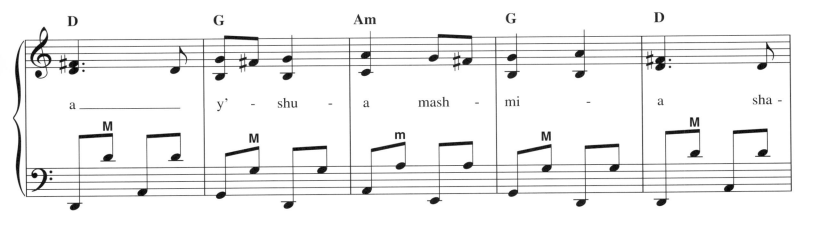

OD YISHAMA
(Again May There Be Heard)

Traditional Jewish Folksong

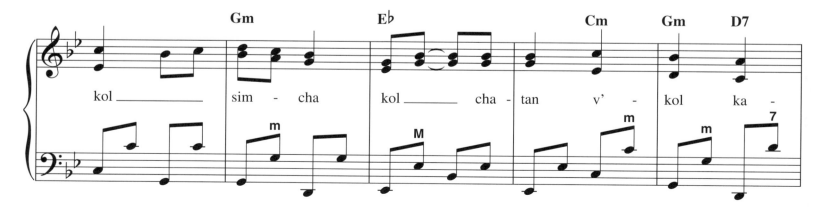

la   od _____ yi - sha - ma b'a - re y'- hu - da

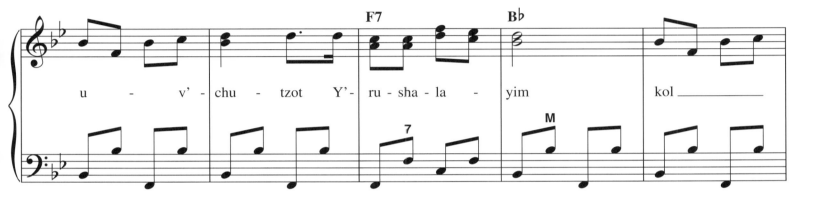

u - v'- chu - tzot Y'- ru - sha - la - yim   kol _____

sa   son v'- kol _____   sim - cha   kol cha - tan v'- kol ___ ka -

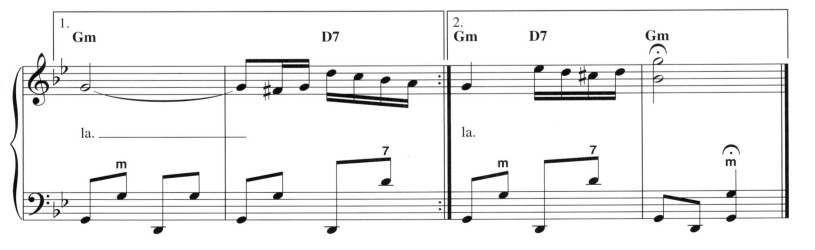

la. _____   la.

SHERELE
(Little Dance)

Traditional Jewish Dance

Quickly

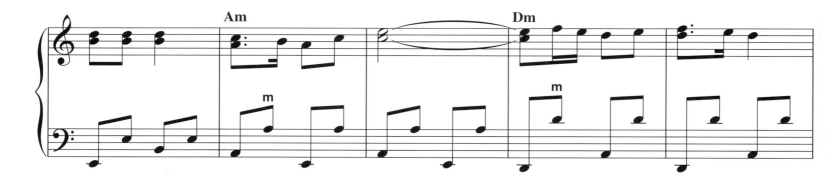

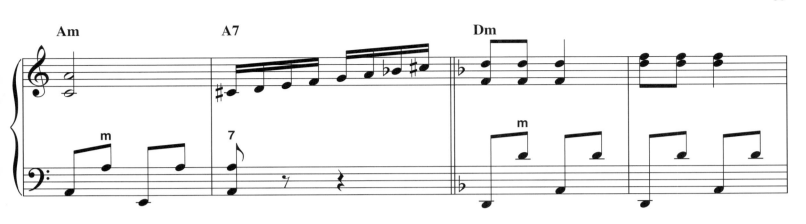

TUM BALALAIKA
(Play the Balalaika)

Yiddish Folksong

Shtét a bo - chur un _____ er tracht tracht un

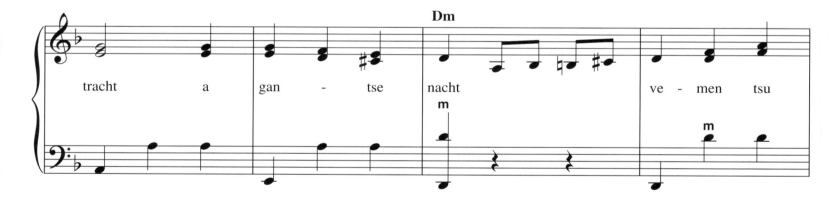

tracht a gan - tse nacht ve - men tsu

ne - men un nit far - shem - en vem - en tsu nem - en

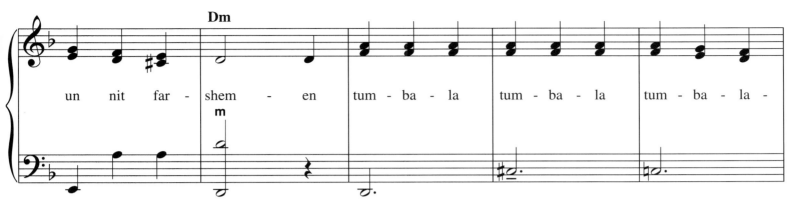

un nit far - shem - en tum - ba - la tum - ba - la tum - ba - la -

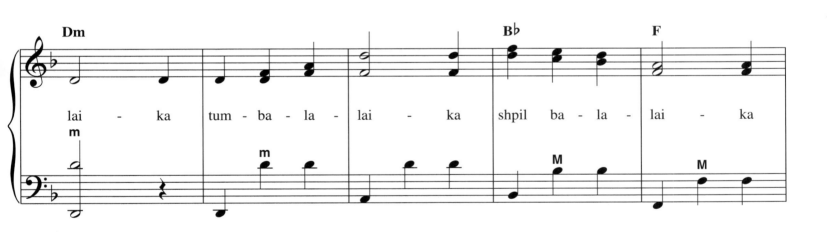

lai - ka tum - ba - la tum - ba - la tum - ba - la -

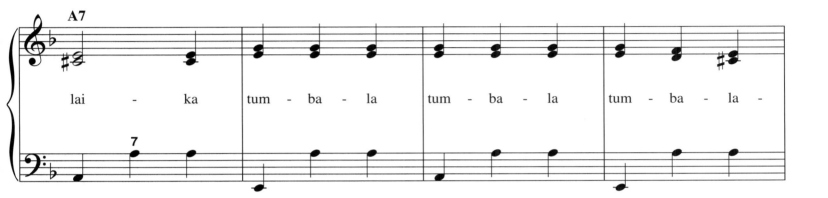

lai - ka tum - ba - la - lai - ka shpil ba - la - lai - ka

shpil ba - la - lai - ka fré - lich zol zain.

SHER
(Dance)

Traditional Jewish Song

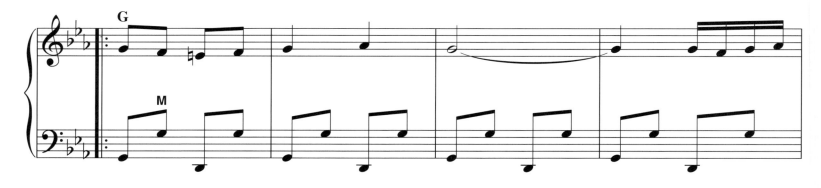

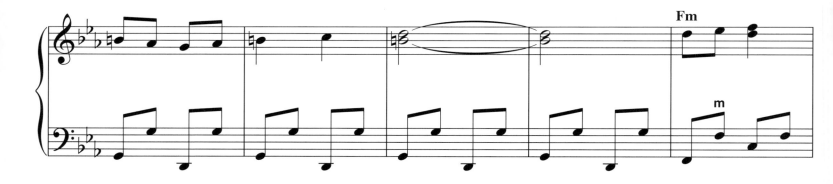

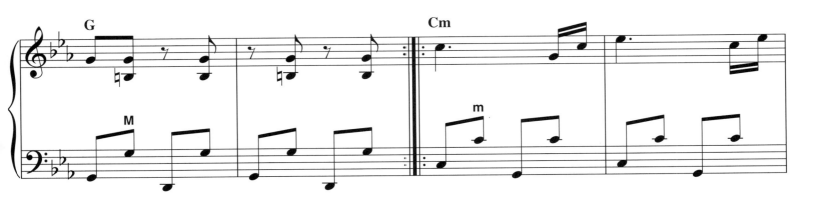

44

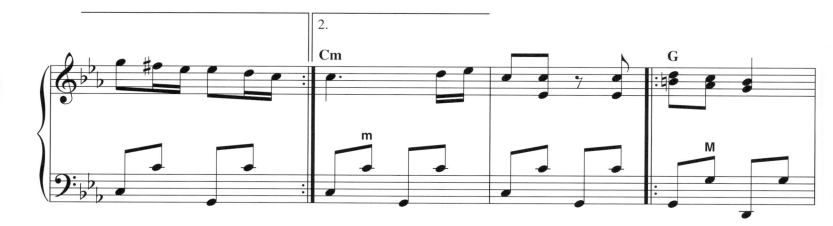

A COLLECTION OF ALL-TIME FAVORITES FOR ACCORDION

ACCORDION FAVORITES
arr. Gary Meisner

16 all-time favorites, arranged for accordion, including: Can't Smile Without You • Could I Have This Dance • Endless Love • Memory • Sunrise, Sunset • I.O.U. • and more.
00359012 ....$10.95

ALL-TIME FAVORITES FOR ACCORDION
arr. Gary Meisner

20 must-know standards arranged for accordions. Includes: Ain't Misbehavin' • Autumn Leaves • Crazy • Hello, Dolly! • Hey, Good Lookin' • Moon River • Speak Softly, Love • Unchained Melody • The Way We Were • Zip-A-Dee-Doo-Dah • and more.
00311088 ....$10.95

THE BEATLES GREATEST HITS FOR ACCORDION

15 of the Beatles greatest hits arranged for accordion. Includes: Lucy in the Sky with Diamonds • A Hard Day's Night • Yellow Submarine • All My Loving • Yesterday • Michelle • Hey Jude • more.
00359121 ....$12.99

BROADWAY FAVORITES
arr. Ken Kotwitz

A collection of 17 wonderful show songs, including: Don't Cry for Me Argentina • Getting to Know You • If I Were a Rich Man • Oklahoma • People Will Say We're in Love • We Kiss in a Shadow.
00490157 ....$9.95

CHRISTMAS SONGS FOR ACCORDION

17 holiday hits, including: The Chipmunk Song • Frosty the Snow Man • A Holly Jolly Christmas • Jingle-Bell Rock • Pretty Paper • Rudolph the Red-Nosed Reindeer.
00359477 ....$8.99

CONTEMPORARY HITS FOR ACCORDION
arr. Gary Meisner

15 songs, including: I Left My Heart in San Francisco • Just the Way You Are • Longer • September Morn • Somewhere Out There • Through the Years • and more.
00359491 ....$9.95

DISNEY MOVIE FAVORITES

Students will love playing these 12 songs from the Disney favorites *Aladdin, Beauty and the Beast*, and *The Little Mermaid*. Songs include: Under the Sea • Be Our Guest • A Whole New World • and more!
00311632 ....$9.95

ITALIAN SONGS FOR ACCORDION
arr. Gary Meisner

17 favorite Italian standards arranged for accordion, including: Carnival of Venice • Ciribiribin • Come Back to Sorrento • Funiculi, Funicula • La donna è mobile • La Spagnola • 'O Sole Mio • Santa Lucia • Tarantella • and more.
00311089 ....$9.95

LATIN FAVORITES FOR ACCORDION
arr. Gary Meisner

20 Latin favorites, including: Bésame Mucho (Kiss Me Much) • The Girl from Ipanema • How Insensitive (Insensatez) • Perfidia • Spanish Eyes • So Nice (Summer Samba) • and more.
00310932 ....$10.99

THE SONGS OF ANDREW LLOYD WEBBER FOR ACCORDION

10 of his best, including: All I Ask of You • Any Dream Will Do • As If We Never Said Goodbye • I Don't Know How to Love Him • Love Changes Everything • The Music of the Night • Old Deuteronomy • Think of Me • Unexpected Song • With One Look.
00310152 ....$10.95

POLKA FAVORITES
arr. Kenny Kotwitz

An exciting new collection of 16 songs, including: Beer Barrel Polka • Liechtensteiner Polka • My Melody of Love • Paloma Blanca • Pennsylvania Polka • Too Fat Polka • and more.
00311573 ....$10.95

WALTZ FAVORITES
arr. Kenny Kotwitz

Accordion arrangements of 17 classic waltzes, including: Alice Blue Gown • I Love You Truly • I Wonder Who's Kissing Her Now • I'll Be with You in Apple Blossom Time • Let Me Call You Sweetheart • Let the Rest of the World Go By • My Buddy • and more.
00310576 ....$9.95

LAWRENCE WELK'S POLKA FOLIO

More than 50 famous polkas, schottisches and waltzes arranged for piano and accordion, including: Blue Eyes • Budweiser Polka • Clarinet Polka • Cuckoo Polka • The Dove Polka • Draw One Polka • Gypsy Polka • Helena Polka • International Waltzes • Let's Have Another One • Schnitzelbank • Shuffle Schottische • Squeeze Box Polka • Waldteufel Waltzes • and more.
00123218 ....$10.95

Prices, contents & availability
subject to change without notice.

Disney artwork & characters © Disney Enterprises, Inc.

FOR MORE INFORMATION,
SEE YOUR LOCAL MUSIC DEALER,
OR WRITE TO:

HAL•LEONARD®
CORPORATION
7777 W. BLUEMOUND RD. P.O. BOX 13819
MILWAUKEE, WISCONSIN 53213

Visit Hal Leonard Online at **www.halleonard.com**